MICHIGAN WOLVERINES

BY K.C. KELLEY

Published by The Child's World®
1980 Lookout Drive • Mankato, MN 56003-1705
800-599-READ • www.childsworld.com

Copyright ©2022 by The Child's World®
All rights reserved. No part of this book may be reproduced or utilized in any form or by any means without written permission from the publisher.

Photos:
Cover and 2: Tom DiPace/AP Images.
Interior: AP Images: Tom Pidgeon 8; Duane Burleson 11, 19; Jon Grau/Icon Sportswire 15; Kevin Reece 16. Newscom: Todd Kirkland/Icon Sportswire 20. Wikimedia: 7 (2); Ken Lund 12.

ISBN 9781503850354 (Reinforced Library Binding)
ISBN 9781503850606 (Portable Document Format)
ISBN 9781503851368 (Online Multi-user eBook)
LCCN: 2021930327

Printed in the United States of America

Michigan players celebrate another touchdown for the Wolverines.

CONTENTS

Why We Love College Football 4

CHAPTER ONE
Early Days 6

CHAPTER TWO
Glory Years 9

CHAPTER THREE
Best Year Ever! 10

CHAPTER FOUR
Michigan Traditions 13

CHAPTER FIVE
Meet the Mascot 14

CHAPTER SIX
Top Michigan QBs 17

CHAPTER SEVEN
Other Michigan Heroes 18

CHAPTER EIGHT
Recent Superstars 21

Glossary 22
Find Out More 23
Index 24

WHY WE LOVE COLLEGE FOOTBALL

The leaves are changing color. Happy crowds fill the stadiums. Pennants wave. And here come the fight songs. It's time for college football! The sport is one of America's most popular. Millions of fans follow their favorite teams. They wear school colors and hope for big wins.

The University of Michigan is one of college football's best. Its long history includes lots of championships. Great players have worn the "maize and blue." Let's meet the famous Wolverines!

The Wolverines play to packed houses in Michigan Stadium in Ann Arbor, Michigan.

CHAPTER ONE

Early Days

Michigan's first game was way back in 1879. They only played two games that season! The first full season came in 1892. Soon, they were one of best teams in the land. They were led by famous coach Fielding Yost. From 1901 to 1918, Michigan never had a **losing record**!

The 1901 team was one of the most successful ever. They won all 11 games. They did not give up a single point! The Wolverines ended the season with a win in the Rose Bowl.

BIG CHANGES

In football's early days, players didn't wear helmets. Games were often very muddy and rough. By the 1920s, new rules helped make the game safer. Players added leather helmets to help protect their heads.

Left: The first Michigan team from 1879.

Below: The 1898 Wolverines were the first to win a conference title.

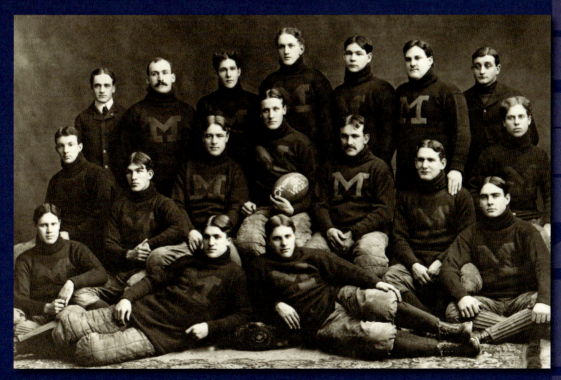

CHAPTER TWO

Glory Years

Michigan has had several periods of greatness. They won back-to-back national titles in 1932 and 1933. Quarterback Harry Newman was the big star. In 1947 and 1948, they did it again! Those teams tried something new. They had players play only defense or offense. Few teams did that in those days!

In the 1970s, Michigan won seven **Big Ten** titles. Rick Leach led the team from 1975 to 1978. His 82 total touchdowns (running and passing) were the most ever to that point by any college player.

ALL-TIME BEST

Michigan has won more games than any other college team. Through 2019, they had 964 wins. The school's 11 national titles are tied for the most, too.

The 1990s were another great time for Michigan. They won five Big Ten titles. The best year was 1997, when they were national champs.

➤ *Why is Michigan's Brian Griese holding a rose? His team just beat rival Ohio State in 1997. Next stop: the Rose Bowl!*

CHAPTER THREE

Best Year Ever!

In 1997, cornerback Charles Woodson led the Wolverines to a perfect 12–0 record. He won the Heisman Trophy. That award is given to college football's best player. He was the first defensive player to win it.

Woodson also returned kicks. He scored TDs on **interception** and **punt returns** and even caught TD passes from quarterback (QB) Brian Griese.

Woodson led a tough defense. They allowed more than 20 points in only one game! Michigan won the Big Ten by beating **rival** Ohio State. Woodson had a punt-return touchdown (TD) in that game. In the Rose Bowl, they beat Washington State 21–16. The Wolverines were number one for the eleventh time!

MICHIGAN'S HEISMAN WINNERS
Tom Harmon, 1940
Desmond Howard, 1991
Charles Woodson, 1997

Ohio State can only watch as Charles Woodson heads to the end zone. *His punt-return TD helped the Wolverines win in 1997.*

The Michigan marching band plays at halftime under the famous Go Blue banner.

CHAPTER FOUR

Michigan Traditions

In more than 140 years, Michigan football has created a lot of traditions! Teams have run under the Go Blue banner since the 1960s.

Michigan has a very famous fight song. *Hail to the Victors* was written in 1898.

> *Hail! to the victors valiant*
> *Hail! to the conqu'ring heroes*
> *Hail! Hail! to Michigan*
> *the champions of the West.*

Why does it say "the West"? Because in those days, Michigan was just about as far west as college football went!

THE BIG RIVAL!

Michigan has two big rivals. The Wolverines battle Michigan State in a cross-state battle. They face Ohio State each year, too. To some fans, Wolverines vs. Buckeyes is college football's biggest rivalry!

CHAPTER FIVE

Meet the Mascot

Wolverines are small but fierce mammals. They live in the woods. They are predators, eating lots of small animals. In the mid-1800s, Michigan became known as the Wolverine State. Using Wolverines as a nickname was a perfect fit for Michigan football!

A stuffed wolverine was the team's mascot for a while. Then they had live wolverines! Biff and Bennie were on the sidelines in the 1920s and 1930s.

THE BIG HOUSE
Michigan plays in the largest stadium in the country. It has seats for more than 107,000 people. At a game in 2013, they squeezed in 115,000! Michigan Stadium was built in 1927. Its nickname is "The Big House."

Michigan does not have a costumed mascot. Instead, a huge cheer squad entertains fans on game day.

Michigan cheerleaders lead the team out while carrying huge flags. Guess what the flags spell out, one letter at a time? ▶

Jim Harbaugh led the Wolverines to a Rose Bowl. In 2015, he became the team's head coach.

CHAPTER SIX

Top Michigan QBs

In the 1920s, Benny Friedman was more than a QB. He was Michigan's kicker and kick returner. He even played defense! Friedman was named to the **All-America** team twice.

Brian Griese led Michigan to a national title in 1997. He was named the most valuable player of the Rose Bowl after throwing three TD passes.

Chad Henne owns most of Michigan's passing records. He played from 2004 to 2007. Henne tossed 87 TDs for 9,715 passing yards. Both are still the most ever for a Wolverine.

Jim Harbaugh was a tough player from 1983 to 1986. As a senior, he threw 18 TD passes and ran for eight scores.

> **A GUY NAMED BRADY**
> Tom Brady has become the greatest QB of all time. Brady was the starting QB at Michigan for two seasons. He led Michigan to two bowl game victories. In the NFL, he won six Super Bowls with the New England Patriots. That's the most ever for a player!

CHAPTER SEVEN

Other Michigan Heroes

Bernie Osterbaan was Michigan's only three-time member of the All-America team. He won the honors in 1925, 1926, and 1927. He was also All-America in basketball and a batting champ in baseball!

Tom Harmon won the 1940 Heisman Trophy. The big runner was known as "Old 98" after his jersey number.

Lineman Steve Hutchinson helped the Wolverines win the title in 1997. He gave up no **sacks** in his final two seasons. "Hutch" played 11 years in the NFL. He was elected to the Pro Football Hall of Fame.

Desmond Howard played wide receiver and returned kicks and punts. In 1991, he set a school record with 21 TDs.

PRESIDENT FOOTBALL

Gerald Ford played center for Michigan from 1932 to 1934. He was a hard-nosed blocker. From 1974 to 1977, he was America's 38th president!

The Iowa player on the ground shouldn't feel bad. No one could stop Heisman winner Desmond Howard in 1991!

CHAPTER EIGHT

Recent Superstars

Michigan reached a bowl game every season but one from 2010 to 2019. Their best season of the **decade** was 2012. They were 11-2 and ranked No. 12. That year, QB Denard Robinson was named a member of the All-America team. Robinson ran for 1,266 yards and seven TDs.

In 2015–16, Michigan had its best **tight end** ever. Jake Butt won two national awards for his position. He set team records for catches by a TE. Jabrill Peppers won the 2016 Ronnie Lott Award as the top **cornerback** in the nation.

In 2019, QB Shea Patterson threw for 3,061 yards. That was the second most in school history.

Who will be the next star to add to Michigan's great history?

— *In 2019, Shea Patterson was a finalist for an award as the nation's top college quarterback.*

GLOSSARY

All-America (ALL uh-MAYR-ih-kuh) an honor given to the top players in college sports

Big Ten (BIG TEN) a conference of 14 colleges that play sports against each other

cornerback (KOR-ner-bak) a defensive position that covers receivers

decade (DEK-ayd) a period of ten years

interception (in-ter-SEP-shun) a pass caught by the defense

lineman (LYNE-man) one of the players who start each play crouching near the ball before it is snapped

losing record (LOO-zing REK-erd) the result of a season in which a team lost more games than it won

punt returns (PUNT ree-TURNZ) plays during which a team catches a punt and runs toward the end zone

rival (RYE-vul) a team faced often over a long period of time

sacks (SAKS) tackles of the quarterback behind the line of scrimmage (where each play starts)

tight end (TYTE END) an offensive position that catches passes and blocks

FIND OUT MORE

IN THE LIBRARY

Jacobs, Greg. *Everything Kids Football Book*. New York: Adams Media, 2015.

Sports Illustrated for Kids. *The Greatest Football Teams of All Time*. New York, NY: Sports Illustrated Kids, 2018.

Weber, Margaret. *Michigan Wolverines*. Calgary, AB: Weigl Publishers, 2019.

ON THE WEB

Visit our website for links about the
Michigan Wolverines:
childsworld.com/links

Note to Parents, Teachers, and Librarians: We routinely verify our Web links to make sure they are safe and active sites. So encourage your readers to check them out!

INDEX

Big Ten, 9, 10
Brady, Tom, 17
Ford, Gerald, 18
Friedman, Benny, 17
Griese, Brian, 9, 10, 17
Harbaugh, Jim, 16, 17
Harmon, Tom, 10, 18
Heisman Trophy, 2, 10, 18
Henne, Chad, 17
Howard, Desmond, 2, 10, 18, 19
Hutchinson, Steve, 18
Leach, Rick, 9
Michigan Stadium, 5, 14
Michigan State, 13
Newman, Harry, 9
Ohio State, 9, 10, 11, 13
Osterbaan, Bernie, 18
Rose Bowl, 6, 9, 10, 16, 17
Super Bowl, 17
Washington State, 10
Woodson, Charles, 10, 11
Yost, Fielding, 6

ABOUT THE AUTHOR

K.C. Kelley is the author of more than 100 sports books for young readers, including numerous biographies of famous athletes. He went to the University of California–Berkeley, but his Golden Bears didn't quite make it into this series!